Private Money Brokering Demystified:

A Step-by-Step Guide for Novice Real Estate Investors

Clyde N. Cook, III ~ The Real Estate Don

Table Of Contents

Chapter 1: Introduction to Private Money Brokering for Residential Real Estate Investments

Understanding the Basics of Private Money Brokering

Private money brokering is a crucial aspect of real estate investments, particularly in the residential sector. For beginning real estate investors, it is essential to grasp the basics of private money brokering to effectively navigate the world of real estate financing. In this subchapter, we will demystify the concept of private money brokering and provide a step-by-step guide for novice real estate investors.

Private money brokering involves connecting real estate investors with private lenders who are willing to finance their projects. Unlike traditional financing options, private money brokering offers flexibility, faster funding, and fewer stringent requirements. This makes it an attractive choice for investors who may not meet the criteria set by banks or traditional lenders.

To get started with private money brokering, it is crucial to understand the key players involved. As a novice real estate investor, you will play the role of the middleman, connecting borrowers with private lenders. Your primary responsibility will be to identify potential borrowers who require funding and match them with suitable private lenders.

One of the critical aspects of private money brokering is building a network of both borrowers and lenders. This network will be your foundation for success in the industry. Building relationships with real estate investors, mortgage brokers, attorneys, and other professionals in the field will help you expand your reach and increase your chances of successful matches.

Another vital aspect of private money brokering is understanding the lending criteria of private lenders. Each lender will have their own set of requirements, such as loan-to-value ratio, credit score criteria, and property type preferences. Being familiar with these criteria will enable you to present potential borrowers who meet the lender's requirements, increasing the likelihood of successful funding.

In addition to understanding the key players and lending criteria, it is essential to learn the art of negotiation and deal structuring. As a private money broker, your role will involve negotiating favorable terms for both parties involved. This includes determining interest rates, loan terms, and any potential fees associated with the transaction.

Lastly, maintaining compliance with legal and ethical guidelines is crucial in private money brokering. Familiarize yourself with local and federal regulations to ensure you operate within the legal boundaries of the industry. This will help build trust with both borrowers and lenders, establishing your reputation as a trustworthy private money broker.

Understanding the basics of private money brokering is a fundamental step for novice real estate investors. By grasping the key players, building a network, understanding lending criteria, mastering negotiation skills, and maintaining compliance, you will be well on your way to becoming a successful private money broker in the residential real estate investment niche.

Benefits of Private Money Brokering for Novice Real Estate Investors

Private money brokering is a thriving industry that offers numerous benefits for novice real estate investors, especially those focused on residential real estate investments. This subchapter explores the advantages of private money brokering and how it can propel beginners towards financial success in the real estate market.

1. Access to Capital: One significant benefit of private money brokering is the access to capital it provides. As a novice real estate investor, securing traditional financing from banks or other financial institutions can be challenging due to limited credit history or lack of collateral. Private money brokering allows investors to tap into a network of private lenders who are willing to provide the necessary funding, even without perfect credit or a large down payment.

2. Flexibility in Terms: Unlike traditional lenders, private money brokers offer flexible loan terms. This means that novice real estate investors can negotiate terms that suit their specific needs and investment strategies. Private lenders are often more open to creative financing options, such as interest-only payments or flexible repayment schedules, providing investors with greater financial flexibility.

3. Faster Approval Process: Private money brokering offers a streamlined approval process compared to traditional lenders. Novice real estate investors can often receive funding within days or weeks, enabling them to act quickly on lucrative investment opportunities. This speed is crucial in a competitive real estate market, where time is of the essence.

4. Nurturing Relationships: Engaging in private money brokering allows novice real estate investors to build relationships with private lenders. These connections can prove invaluable in the long run, as they can lead to additional funding for future projects. Building a strong network of private lenders who trust and believe in your investment strategies can pave the way for continued success and growth.

5. Expand Investment Opportunities: Private money brokering opens up a world of investment opportunities that may not be accessible through traditional financing methods. With private lenders, novice real estate investors can explore unconventional projects, such as fix-and-flip properties or distressed real estate, without being limited by strict lending criteria.

In conclusion, private money brokering offers numerous benefits to novice real estate investors in the residential real estate niche. The access to capital, flexibility in terms, faster approval process, nurturing relationships, and expanded investment opportunities make private money brokering an attractive option for those starting out in real estate investing. By leveraging these advantages, beginners can accelerate their journey towards financial success and achieve their real estate investment goals.

Common Misconceptions about Private Money Brokering

As a beginning real estate investor venturing into the world of private money brokering for residential real estate investments, it is important to address and debunk some common misconceptions surrounding this field. Private money brokering may seem intimidating and complex at first, but understanding the truth behind these misconceptions will help you navigate this exciting landscape with confidence and clarity.

Misconception 1: Private Money Brokering is Only for Experienced Investors

One of the biggest misconceptions about private money brokering is that it is exclusively reserved for seasoned investors. In reality, anyone with a passion for real estate and a willingness to learn can become a successful private money broker. The key is to educate yourself about the industry, build relationships with potential lenders, and develop a solid understanding of the loan process.

Misconception 2: Private Money Brokering Requires a Large Network

While having a strong network can certainly be beneficial, it is not a prerequisite for success in private money brokering. With the advent of technology and social media, it is easier than ever to connect with potential lenders and expand your network. Additionally, there are numerous online platforms and forums dedicated to private money brokering, providing opportunities to connect with like-minded individuals and potential investors.

Misconception 3: Private Money Brokering is Risky

Another misconception surrounding private money brokering is that it involves high levels of risk. While there are risks associated with any investment, proper due diligence and risk assessment can minimize these risks significantly. As a private money broker, it is your responsibility to thoroughly vet potential lenders and evaluate the viability of their investment opportunities. By conducting thorough research and building a robust network of trusted lenders, you can mitigate the risks involved in private money brokering.

Misconception 4: Private Money Brokering is Time-Consuming

Contrary to popular belief, private money brokering does not necessarily require a significant amount of time. With the right systems and processes in place, you can streamline your operations and effectively manage your time. Automation tools and software can simplify tasks such as document management, lead generation, and communication, allowing you to focus on building relationships and closing deals.

In conclusion, private money brokering for residential real estate investments is not as daunting as it may initially seem. By dispelling these common misconceptions, beginning real estate investors can confidently embark on their journey into the world of private money brokering. With a solid understanding of the industry, a willingness to learn, and a commitment to building relationships, success in private money brokering is within reach.

Chapter 2: Getting Started in Private Money Brokering

Assessing Your Financial Goals and Objectives

As a beginning real estate investor venturing into the world of private money brokering for residential real estate investments, it is crucial to have a clear understanding of your financial goals and objectives. This subchapter aims to guide you through the process of assessing and defining your financial goals, enabling you to pave a path towards success in the realm of real estate.

Setting goals is an essential first step in any endeavor, and real estate investing is no exception. By identifying your financial goals, you can align your efforts and resources to achieve them efficiently. Start by asking yourself what you hope to accomplish through your real estate investments. Are you looking to generate passive income, build long-term wealth, or diversify your investment portfolio? Understanding your ultimate objective will help you make informed decisions along the way.

Once you have a clear vision of your goals, it is important to establish specific, measurable, attainable, relevant, and time-bound (SMART) objectives. For instance, if your goal is to generate a passive income of $5,000 per month from real estate investments, you can set specific objectives such as acquiring three rental properties within the next two years with an average monthly cash flow of $1,500 each. These specific objectives provide a roadmap for your actions and give you a sense of direction.

In addition to setting specific objectives, it is crucial to assess your risk tolerance and financial capacity. Real estate investments come with inherent risks, and understanding your comfort level with these risks is essential. Evaluate your financial resources, including the amount of capital you can invest, your creditworthiness, and your ability to secure funding. This assessment will enable you to make realistic financial decisions and avoid overextending yourself.

Furthermore, it is essential to consider your time commitment and personal preferences. Real estate investments require active management, including property maintenance, tenant management, and financial tracking. Assessing how much time you can dedicate to these responsibilities will help you determine the scale and type of investments that align with your lifestyle.

By assessing your financial goals and objectives, you lay a solid foundation for your journey into private money brokering for residential real estate investments. This self-reflection and planning process will guide your decision-making and ensure that your investments are aligned with your long-term vision. Remember to regularly review and adjust your goals and objectives as your circumstances and market conditions evolve, allowing you to stay on track towards achieving financial success in the real estate industry.

Building Your Real Estate Network

One of the most crucial aspects of success in the real estate industry is building a strong and reliable network. As a beginning real estate investor, establishing and nurturing your network is vital for your growth in private money brokering for residential real estate investments. In this subchapter, we will delve into the various strategies and techniques to help you build a robust real estate network.

Firstly, it is important to understand the significance of networking in the real estate world. Your network will consist of individuals who can provide you with valuable resources, information, and potential investment opportunities. These individuals may include other real estate investors, real estate agents, mortgage brokers, contractors, attorneys, and property managers. By connecting with these professionals, you can tap into their expertise and leverage their network to enhance your own.

To start building your network, attend local real estate networking events and join industry-specific groups or organizations. These events and groups provide an excellent opportunity to meet like-minded individuals and establish meaningful connections. Actively participate in discussions, share your knowledge, and seek advice from experienced investors. Remember, networking is a two-way street, so be willing to offer assistance and value to others as well.

Utilize online platforms and social media to expand your network beyond physical boundaries. Join real estate forums and engage in discussions on platforms such as BiggerPockets, LinkedIn, and Facebook groups dedicated to real estate investing. These platforms allow you to connect with professionals from all over the world, learn from their experiences, and gain valuable insights into the industry.

Additionally, consider forming strategic partnerships with other investors or professionals in complementary fields. For instance, partnering with a real estate agent can provide you with access to off-market deals, while teaming up with a contractor can help streamline the renovation process. By combining your skills and resources, you can maximize your potential for success.

Networking is not limited to professionals within the real estate industry. Don't overlook the importance of building relationships with potential private money lenders. Attend local investment club meetings or real estate seminars to connect with potential private lenders who may be interested in funding your residential real estate investments.

Lastly, always remember to nurture and maintain your network. Regularly follow up with individuals you meet, offer assistance whenever possible, and keep them informed about your progress. Building a strong network requires continuous effort and dedication, so be proactive in fostering these relationships.

In conclusion, building your real estate network is a fundamental step for beginning real estate investors looking to venture into private money brokering for residential real estate investments. By actively participating in networking events, utilizing online platforms, forming strategic partnerships, and connecting with potential private money lenders, you can establish a robust network that will provide you with valuable resources, opportunities, and support on your investment journey.

Establishing Credibility and Trust

In the world of real estate investing, establishing credibility and trust is paramount to success. As a beginning real estate investor looking to delve into the niche of private money brokering for residential real estate investments, it is crucial to understand the importance of building a solid foundation of credibility and trust with potential private money lenders.

Private money brokering involves connecting real estate investors with private individuals or companies willing to lend money for their investment projects. These lenders are looking for trustworthy individuals who can demonstrate their ability to effectively manage and generate returns on their investments. Therefore, gaining their confidence is key to securing the necessary funds for your residential real estate ventures.

One of the first steps in establishing credibility and trust is to educate yourself about the real estate market and investment strategies. By becoming knowledgeable about the industry, you can speak confidently and intelligently with potential lenders, showing them that you are well-prepared and serious about your investments.

Additionally, networking plays a crucial role in building credibility. Attend real estate investment conferences, seminars, and local meetups to connect with experienced investors and industry professionals. By associating yourself with credible individuals, you can gain valuable insights and establish yourself as a serious player in the field.

Maintaining a professional online presence is another essential aspect of establishing credibility. Create a professional website or blog where you can showcase your previous successful investments, market expertise, and testimonials from satisfied clients. Being active on social media platforms, such as LinkedIn and Facebook, can also help you connect with potential lenders and showcase your knowledge and experience.

Furthermore, transparency and honesty are vital in developing trust with private money lenders. Clearly communicate your investment strategies, risks, and potential returns, ensuring that lenders are fully aware of the details of the investment opportunity. This transparency will not only establish trust but also help you attract lenders who align with your investment goals.

Lastly, consistently delivering on your promises is crucial for building a solid reputation. By executing successful investment projects and generating positive returns for your lenders, you will solidify your credibility and trustworthiness in the eyes of potential future lenders.

Establishing credibility and trust in private money brokering for residential real estate investments is a gradual process. However, by continuously educating yourself, networking, maintaining a professional online presence, being transparent, and consistently delivering results, you can build a strong foundation of credibility and trust, paving the way for successful real estate investment ventures.

Chapter 3: Finding Private Money Lenders

Understanding the Role of Private Money Lenders in Real Estate Investing

Private money lenders play a crucial role in the world of real estate investing, especially for beginning investors looking to finance their residential property ventures. In this subchapter, we will delve into the importance of private money lenders, how they differ from traditional lenders, and how novice real estate investors can benefit from their services.

Private money lenders, also known as hard money lenders, are individuals or companies that provide loans to real estate investors for the purpose of purchasing and renovating residential properties. Unlike traditional lenders such as banks or mortgage companies, private money lenders base their lending decisions on the value of the property and the investor's ability to make a profit, rather than solely relying on credit scores and income verification. This makes private money lending a more viable option for novice real estate investors who may not have established credit or a substantial income history.

One of the key advantages of working with private money lenders is the speed at which they can provide financing. Traditional lenders often have lengthy approval processes that can delay a real estate investment project. In contrast, private money lenders can typically approve and fund a loan within a matter of days, allowing investors to seize time-sensitive opportunities in the market. This flexibility is especially important for beginning investors who may need to act quickly to secure a property.

Furthermore, private money lenders are often more willing to finance unconventional projects or properties that may not meet the stringent requirements of traditional lenders. This opens up a world of possibilities for novice investors, allowing them to explore unique investment opportunities and potentially earn higher returns.

However, it is important for beginning real estate investors to thoroughly research and vet potential private money lenders before entering into any financial agreements. Due diligence should include evaluating the lender's experience, reputation, interest rates, loan terms, and fees. Building relationships with reputable private money lenders can provide a steady source of funding for future real estate investment projects.

In conclusion, private money lenders play a vital role in the world of real estate investing, particularly for beginning investors. Their ability to provide quick financing, flexibility in approving unconventional projects, and focus on the property's potential profitability make them valuable partners for those seeking to build a real estate investment portfolio. By understanding and leveraging the services of private money lenders, novice real estate investors can gain a competitive edge and unlock a myriad of opportunities in the residential real estate market.

Identifying Potential Private Money Lenders

As a beginning real estate investor, one of the most crucial skills you need to master is the art of securing financing for your residential real estate investments. While traditional lenders may be a viable option, they often come with stringent requirements and lengthy approval processes. This is where private money lenders come in, offering a faster and more flexible alternative for funding your real estate ventures. But how do you go about identifying potential private money lenders? Let's delve into the key strategies you can employ.

1. Networking: Building a strong network is paramount in the world of private money brokering. Attend real estate investment clubs, industry conferences, and local networking events to connect with potential lenders. Engage in meaningful conversations, share your investment goals, and listen attentively to others' experiences. Building relationships will help you identify individuals who may be interested in becoming private money lenders.

2. Real Estate Professionals: Reach out to real estate agents, brokers, and property managers who have a deep understanding of the local market. These professionals often have connections with private money lenders or may even be lenders themselves. By collaborating with them, you not only gain invaluable insights into the market but also increase your chances of finding potential lenders.

3. Online Platforms: Utilize online platforms and forums dedicated to private money lending. Websites like BiggerPockets, Connected Investors, and PrivateLenderLink connect real estate investors with private lenders. Create a compelling profile, clearly outlining your investment goals and experience, and actively engage with other members. These platforms provide an excellent avenue for connecting with potential private money lenders from around the country.

4. Professional Associations: Join professional associations and organizations related to real estate investing. These groups often have members who are experienced private money lenders or have access to a network of lenders. Attend association meetings, participate in discussions, and contribute your knowledge. By actively engaging with these communities, you increase your visibility and the likelihood of finding potential lenders.

5. Local Business Directories: Explore local business directories and search for companies that specialize in private lending or alternative financing. These companies are often willing to work with real estate investors and may have a pool of private money lenders they can connect you with.

Remember, when identifying potential private money lenders, it's essential to establish trust and credibility. Be transparent about your investment plans, financial situation, and exit strategies. Always conduct thorough due diligence on potential lenders, verifying their track record, reputation, and terms offered. By employing these strategies and consistently expanding your network, you'll be well on your way to finding the ideal private money lenders to support your residential real estate investments.

Approaching and Building Relationships with Private Money Lenders

One of the most crucial aspects of private money brokering for residential real estate investments is establishing and nurturing relationships with private money lenders. These individuals or organizations can be a valuable source of funding for your real estate ventures, providing you with the capital needed to acquire and develop properties. In this subchapter, we will delve into the strategies and best practices for approaching and building relationships with private money lenders.

Firstly, it is important to understand that private money lenders are not as easily accessible as traditional financial institutions. They operate outside the realm of banks and credit unions, making it essential for beginning real estate investors to actively seek out these lenders. One effective approach is to attend local real estate networking events, where you can connect with potential private money lenders who are interested in investing in residential real estate projects. Additionally, leveraging online platforms and forums dedicated to real estate investing can help you identify and connect with private money lenders.

Once you have identified potential lenders, the next step is to build a rapport and establish trust. Remember, private money lenders are entrusting their capital to you, so it is crucial to present yourself as a knowledgeable and reliable individual. Prepare a compelling pitch that showcases your experience, expertise, and the potential returns on investment. It is also important to emphasize the security and profitability of residential real estate investments, highlighting your due diligence in analyzing properties and mitigating risks.

To strengthen your relationship with private money lenders, it is essential to maintain regular communication. Keep them updated on your ongoing projects, providing progress reports and financial statements to instill confidence in their investment. Additionally, consider establishing a personal connection by taking the time to understand their investment goals, preferences, and risk tolerance. This will allow you to tailor your investment proposals to align with their specific requirements, increasing the likelihood of securing funding for your real estate ventures.

Lastly, building a network of private money lenders is an ongoing process. Continuously seek out new opportunities to connect with potential lenders, whether it be through industry events, online platforms, or referrals from existing lenders. Remember, private money lenders are often well-connected individuals who can introduce you to other potential lenders, expanding your network and funding options.

Approaching and building relationships with private money lenders is a pivotal step in becoming a successful private money broker for residential real estate investments. By actively seeking out lenders, building trust, maintaining regular communication, and expanding your network, you can secure the necessary capital to thrive in the real estate industry.

Chapter 4: Understanding Private Money Loans

Types of Private Money Loans

In the world of real estate investing, securing funds for your residential property ventures can often be a daunting task, especially for novice investors. Traditional lending institutions may not always be the best option due to their stringent requirements and lengthy approval processes. This is where private money loans come into play. Private money loans, also known as hard money loans, are an alternative financing option that can help beginning real estate investors overcome the hurdles of obtaining funding.

There are various types of private money loans available, each tailored to suit different investment needs. Understanding these options is essential for novice investors looking to enter the world of real estate and private money brokering. Let's explore the different types of private money loans commonly used in residential real estate investments.

1. Fix and Flip Loans: This type of loan is ideal for investors looking to purchase distressed properties, renovate them, and sell them for a profit. Fix and flip loans typically have shorter terms, higher interest rates, and are based on the property's after-repair value (ARV).

2. Rental Property Loans: Designed for investors who want to build a portfolio of rental properties, these loans provide funds to purchase and renovate properties that will generate rental income. Rental property loans have longer terms and lower interest rates compared to fix and flip loans.

3. Bridge Loans: Bridge loans are short-term financing options that bridge the gap between the purchase of a new property and the sale of an existing one. These loans help investors avoid missing out on a lucrative investment opportunity due to timing constraints.

4. Construction Loans: Investors looking to build or renovate properties from the ground up can benefit from construction loans. These loans are disbursed in stages based on the completion of specific construction milestones.

5. Land Loans: Land loans are used to purchase undeveloped land for future residential development. This type of loan is typically secured by the land itself and may have higher interest rates and shorter terms.

Understanding these different types of private money loans is crucial for beginning real estate investors. By choosing the right loan for their investment strategy, investors can leverage private money to fund their residential real estate ventures successfully. Whether it's flipping properties, generating rental income, or building from scratch, private money loans offer flexible and accessible financing options for those willing to explore this alternative route. As a novice investor, taking the time to educate yourself on private money brokering will empower you to make informed decisions and maximize your real estate investment opportunities.

Loan Terms and Conditions

As a beginning real estate investor venturing into private money brokering for residential real estate investments, it is crucial to understand the various loan terms and conditions that come into play. These terms and conditions not only shape the structure of the loan but also impact your investment strategy and overall profitability. In this subchapter, we will delve into the key aspects of loan terms and conditions to equip you with the necessary knowledge for successful private money brokering.

1. Interest Rates: One of the most critical aspects of any loan is the interest rate. As a beginner, it is vital to understand the difference between fixed and variable interest rates. A fixed interest rate remains constant throughout the loan tenure, providing stability and predictability. On the other hand, a variable interest rate fluctuates with market conditions, potentially offering lower rates initially but exposing you to interest rate risk.

2. Loan Duration: The loan duration, commonly referred to as the term, determines the period over which you will repay the loan. Shorter-term loans may offer lower interest rates but require higher monthly payments, while longer-term loans provide lower monthly payments but often come with higher interest rates. It is crucial to find the right balance that aligns with your investment goals and cash flow projections.

3. Loan-to-Value Ratio (LTV): LTV is a critical factor that determines the maximum amount of financing you can obtain compared to the property's value. Lenders typically have LTV limits, and understanding these restrictions is vital when structuring your real estate investments. A higher LTV may provide more flexibility but could come with higher interest rates or additional requirements, such as mortgage insurance.

4. Prepayment Penalties: Prepayment penalties are charges imposed by lenders if you decide to pay off the loan early. As a beginner, it is essential to carefully review the prepayment penalty terms, as they can significantly impact your ability to refinance or sell the property before the loan term ends. Negotiating or selecting loans without prepayment penalties can provide you with more flexibility and potential cost savings.

5. Collateral Requirements: Private lenders often require collateral for the loan, typically in the form of the property itself. Understanding the lender's collateral requirements is crucial to ensure that your investment property qualifies and to anticipate any potential challenges or additional costs associated with appraisal or title searches.

By comprehending these loan terms and conditions, you will be better equipped to navigate the private money brokering landscape for residential real estate investments. It is essential to carefully review and compare loan offerings from various lenders to find the best fit for your investment strategy and financial goals. Remember, thorough due diligence and a clear understanding of loan terms and conditions are key to your success as a beginning real estate investor in private money brokering.

Evaluating the Risks and Rewards of Private Money Loans

As a beginning real estate investor looking to venture into private money brokering for residential real estate investments, it is crucial to understand and evaluate the risks and rewards associated with private money loans. Private money loans, also known as hard money loans or bridge loans, are often provided by private individuals or companies rather than traditional lending institutions like banks. They can offer a flexible and efficient financing option for real estate investors, but it's essential to carefully assess the potential risks and rewards before diving in.

One significant advantage of private money loans is the speed at which they can be obtained. Unlike traditional lenders, private money lenders rely less on credit scores and more on the value of the property itself. This allows for a faster approval process, enabling investors to secure financing quickly, which is especially beneficial in competitive real estate markets.

Private money loans also offer more flexibility than traditional loans. They can be tailored to meet the specific needs of the investor and the property being financed. This flexibility can be advantageous when dealing with distressed properties or properties that require significant renovations before they can be resold or rented out.

However, it is crucial to recognize the potential risks involved with private money loans. Since private lenders take on higher risks, they typically charge higher interest rates than traditional lenders. This can impact the overall profitability of your investment, especially if the property takes longer to sell or rent than anticipated. Additionally, the shorter repayment terms of private money loans may require you to have a well-defined exit strategy to ensure timely repayment.

Another risk to consider is the potential for fraudulent or unscrupulous lenders in the private money lending industry. As a novice real estate investor, it is essential to conduct thorough due diligence on any potential private money lenders. Research their reputation, check for any complaints or legal issues, and seek recommendations from trusted sources before entering into any loan agreements.

In conclusion, evaluating the risks and rewards of private money loans is a crucial step for beginning real estate investors looking to explore private money brokering for residential real estate investments. While private money loans offer speed and flexibility, they also come with higher interest rates and potential risks. By conducting proper due diligence and understanding the terms and conditions of private money loans, investors can make informed decisions and maximize their chances of success in the real estate market.

Chapter 5: Creating a Winning Real Estate Investment Proposal

Essentials of a Real Estate Investment Proposal

When it comes to real estate investing, having a solid investment proposal is essential to attract private money lenders and secure funding for your residential real estate projects. A well-crafted proposal not only showcases your investment opportunity but also instills confidence in potential investors. In this subchapter, we will delve into the essentials of a real estate investment proposal, providing you with the necessary tools to create a compelling document that will impress private money lenders.

1. Executive Summary: Begin your investment proposal with a concise executive summary that highlights the key details of your project. This section should include an overview of the investment opportunity, the expected return on investment, and a brief description of your experience and expertise in the real estate industry.

2. Property Analysis: Provide a detailed analysis of the property you intend to invest in. Include information such as location, market trends, property value, potential rental income, and any renovations or improvements required. Use data and statistics to support your analysis and demonstrate the profitability of the investment.

3. Investment Strategy: Clearly outline your investment strategy, including your goals, timeline, and exit strategy. Discuss whether you plan to buy and hold the property for rental income, flip it for a quick profit, or engage in other real estate investment strategies. This section should demonstrate your knowledge of the market and your ability to generate substantial returns.

4. Financial Projections: Provide a comprehensive financial projection that includes the expected costs, revenues, and profitability of the investment. Include a breakdown of expenses, such as purchase price, renovation costs, holding costs, and potential rental income. Utilize realistic assumptions and provide a clear timeline for the projected returns on investment.

5. Risk Assessment: Address any potential risks associated with the investment and demonstrate your ability to mitigate them. Discuss factors such as market fluctuations, competition, regulatory changes, and potential maintenance or repair issues. Show that you have considered these risks and have a plan to overcome them.

6. Exit Strategy: Outline your exit strategy, detailing how you plan to liquidate the investment and provide a return to your investors. Discuss potential options such as selling the property, refinancing, or offering a buyout to your private money lenders. This section should demonstrate that you have a well-thought-out plan to ensure a successful exit from the investment.

By including these essential elements in your real estate investment proposal, you will be able to effectively communicate your investment opportunity to potential private money lenders. Remember to tailor your proposal to the specific needs and preferences of your target audience, highlighting the benefits and potential returns they can expect from investing in your residential real estate projects. With a compelling investment proposal, you will be well on your way to securing the necessary funding to kickstart your real estate investment journey.

Presenting Your Investment Proposal to Private Money Lenders

One of the key components of successful private money brokering for residential real estate investments is the ability to present your investment proposal effectively to private money lenders. This subchapter will guide beginning real estate investors on how to present their investment proposals in a way that captures the attention of private money lenders and increases the chances of securing funding.

First and foremost, it is crucial to thoroughly research and analyze the property you are looking to invest in. This includes conducting a comprehensive market analysis, evaluating the property's potential for appreciation, and assessing any potential risks or challenges. By presenting a well-researched investment opportunity, you will demonstrate your expertise and competence to potential lenders.

Next, you need to create a compelling investment proposal that effectively communicates the potential return on investment (ROI) to private money lenders. This includes providing detailed financial projections, such as cash flow analysis, estimated expenses, and projected profits. Additionally, you should highlight any unique selling points of the property, such as its location, amenities, or potential for value-add improvements.

When presenting your investment proposal, it is important to be confident, concise, and persuasive. You should clearly articulate your investment strategy, including your plans for acquiring the property, managing it, and eventually selling it for a profit. Emphasize your expertise and track record in real estate investing, if applicable, to instill trust and confidence in the lender.

To further strengthen your investment proposal, consider including a thorough exit strategy. Private money lenders are particularly interested in how and when they will be repaid. Outline your plans for repaying the loan, whether it is through selling the property, refinancing, or other means. This will alleviate any concerns lenders may have regarding the return of their investment.

Finally, it is essential to establish a personal connection with private money lenders. Building relationships with potential lenders can significantly increase your chances of securing funding. Attend real estate networking events, join local investor groups, and actively engage with potential lenders. By establishing a rapport and demonstrating your commitment to success, you will stand out from other investors and leave a lasting impression.

In conclusion, presenting your investment proposal to private money lenders is a critical step in securing funding for residential real estate investments. By conducting thorough research, creating a compelling investment proposal, and establishing personal connections, beginning real estate investors can increase their chances of successfully securing private money lending for their investment projects.

Negotiating Loan Terms and Conditions

As a beginning real estate investor, one of the most crucial skills you need to acquire is the ability to negotiate favorable loan terms and conditions. This subchapter will guide you through the process of negotiating with private money lenders for residential real estate investments.

When it comes to private money brokering for residential real estate investments, understanding the loan terms and conditions is essential. These terms will determine the cost of borrowing, repayment schedule, and overall feasibility of your investment. Here are some key points to consider when negotiating loan terms and conditions:

1. Interest Rates: Start by researching current market rates for similar loans. This will give you a benchmark to negotiate from. Remember, private money lenders often charge higher interest rates than traditional lenders. However, there may be room for negotiation based on factors such as the property's potential return on investment or your personal creditworthiness.

2. Loan Duration: Determine the ideal duration for your loan. Short-term loans are suitable for quick fix-and-flip projects, while long-term loans work better for buy-and-hold strategies. Negotiate a duration that aligns with your investment goals and exit strategy.

3. Repayment Schedule: Discuss the repayment schedule with your lender. Some lenders may require monthly payments, while others may prefer a lump sum payment at the end of the loan term. Negotiate a schedule that suits your cash flow and investment strategy.

4. Loan-to-Value (LTV) Ratio: Private lenders typically offer a percentage of the property's value as a loan. Negotiate the LTV ratio to ensure you have enough funds for your investment while balancing the lender's risk tolerance.

5. Prepayment Penalties: Determine if there are any prepayment penalties included in the loan terms. Negotiate for flexibility in case you decide to sell the property earlier than anticipated or refinance the loan.

6. Collateral Requirements: Private lenders often require collateral to secure the loan. Negotiate the type and value of collateral required, ensuring it aligns with the property's value and your risk tolerance.

7. Miscellaneous Fees: Discuss and negotiate any additional fees associated with the loan, such as origination fees, appraisal fees, or underwriting fees. Be sure to have a clear understanding of all costs involved before finalizing the loan.

Remember, negotiating loan terms and conditions is a skill that improves with experience. Be prepared to ask for what you want while considering the lender's perspective. By understanding the key factors and effectively negotiating, you can secure favorable loan terms that support your residential real estate investments and help you achieve your financial goals.

Chapter 6: Managing Your Private Money Brokering Business

Building a Professional Reputation in the Industry

As a beginning real estate investor looking to venture into private money brokering for residential real estate investments, building a professional reputation in the industry is crucial to your success. The way you are perceived by others can greatly impact your ability to attract potential lenders and investors. In this subchapter, we will discuss some key strategies for establishing and maintaining a strong professional reputation.

First and foremost, it is essential to conduct yourself with integrity and honesty in all your dealings. Trust is the foundation of any successful business relationship, and this holds true in the world of private money brokering. Always be transparent about the risks and rewards involved in an investment opportunity, and never make promises you cannot deliver on. By demonstrating your commitment to ethical practices, you will earn the respect and trust of your clients and colleagues.

Networking is another crucial aspect of building a professional reputation. Attend industry events, join real estate investment clubs, and actively seek out opportunities to connect with experienced investors and lenders. Building relationships with these individuals can open doors to potential partnerships and private funding sources. Remember, networking is not just about what others can do for you, but also about what you can bring to the table. Be generous with your time and knowledge, and always be willing to help others in the industry.

In addition to networking, it is important to establish yourself as an expert in your field. Stay up-to-date with the latest trends and developments in private money brokering and residential real estate investments. Share your knowledge through writing articles, starting a blog, or even hosting educational webinars. By positioning yourself as a thought leader, you will gain credibility and attract potential clients who value your expertise.

Lastly, never underestimate the power of testimonials and referrals. Satisfied clients are more likely to recommend your services to others, so always strive to exceed their expectations. Ask for testimonials and display them on your website or promotional materials. Additionally, consider offering referral incentives to encourage satisfied clients to refer new business your way.

In conclusion, building a professional reputation in the industry is vital for beginning real estate investors looking to enter the world of private money brokering for residential real estate investments. Conducting yourself with integrity, networking, establishing yourself as an expert, and leveraging testimonials and referrals are all key strategies to help you succeed in this competitive field. By following these guidelines, you will not only attract potential lenders and investors but also establish yourself as a trusted and respected professional in the industry.

Developing Effective Marketing Strategies

When it comes to private money brokering for residential real estate investments, developing effective marketing strategies is crucial for success. As a beginning real estate investor, understanding how to attract potential lenders and build a network of private money sources is essential to fund your real estate deals. In this subchapter, we will explore some key strategies that will help you develop a strong marketing plan for your private money brokering business.

First and foremost, it is important to identify your target audience. Knowing who your potential lenders are will allow you to tailor your marketing efforts towards their specific needs and preferences. Consider the characteristics of your ideal lender, such as their investment goals, risk tolerance, and desired return on investment. This will help you create targeted marketing materials that resonate with your target audience.

One effective marketing strategy is to establish a strong online presence. Building a professional website and utilizing social media platforms will allow you to reach a wider audience and showcase your expertise in private money brokering. Create informative content that educates potential lenders about the benefits of investing in residential real estate and how you can help them achieve their financial goals.

Networking is another powerful marketing tool in the private money brokering industry. Attend real estate conferences, join local real estate investment clubs, and actively participate in online communities to connect with potential lenders. Building relationships and establishing trust is key in this business, so make sure to follow up regularly with your contacts and provide value through networking events or educational resources.

In addition to online marketing and networking, traditional marketing methods should not be overlooked. Consider distributing flyers, business cards, or brochures at local real estate events or even in targeted neighborhoods. Direct mail campaigns can also be effective in reaching potential lenders who may not be active online.

Lastly, tracking and analyzing your marketing efforts is crucial to measure their effectiveness. Use analytics tools to monitor website traffic, email open rates, and conversion rates. This data will help you identify which marketing strategies are bringing in the most leads and make adjustments accordingly.

In conclusion, developing effective marketing strategies is essential for private money brokering success in residential real estate investments. By identifying your target audience, building an online presence, networking, utilizing traditional marketing methods, and tracking your efforts, you will be well on your way to attracting potential lenders and growing your private money brokering business.

Managing the Deal Flow and Loan Processing

As a beginning real estate investor, one of the most crucial aspects of your success in private money brokering for residential real estate investments is effectively managing the deal flow and loan processing. This subchapter will guide you through the essential steps and strategies to ensure a smooth and efficient process.

Deal flow refers to the number of potential investment opportunities that come your way. It's important to establish a system to effectively manage and evaluate these deals to ensure you are investing in the most profitable and suitable properties. Start by creating a clear criteria checklist that outlines your investment goals, desired property types, locations, and financial parameters. This will help you quickly filter out irrelevant opportunities and focus on the most promising ones.

Additionally, networking plays a crucial role in expanding your deal flow. Attend real estate investment clubs, industry conferences, and connect with other investors and professionals in the real estate field. Building a strong network will not only increase your deal flow but also provide valuable insights and opportunities for collaboration.

Once you've identified a potential investment opportunity, the loan processing phase comes into play. This involves securing the necessary financing for your real estate investment. It's essential to establish relationships with reliable lenders and private money sources who understand your investment strategy and are willing to provide funding.

When working with lenders, be prepared to provide detailed information about the property, its potential returns, and your own financial position. This includes property appraisals, market analysis, and your personal financial statements. By providing a comprehensive package, you increase your chances of securing the loan quickly and at favorable terms.

Furthermore, having a thorough understanding of the loan processing timeline is crucial. Each lender has their own set of requirements and processing timeframes, so it's vital to establish clear communication channels and follow-up regularly. This ensures that you are aware of any additional documentation needed and can address any potential issues promptly.

To streamline the loan processing phase, consider leveraging technology and digital tools. Many lenders now offer online platforms for loan applications and document submissions, making the process more efficient and convenient.

In conclusion, managing the deal flow and loan processing is a critical aspect of private money brokering for residential real estate investments. By establishing clear criteria, expanding your network, and building strong relationships with lenders, you can effectively evaluate investment opportunities and secure favorable financing. Remember to stay organized, communicate proactively, and leverage technology to streamline the process and maximize your chances of success.

Chapter 7: Ensuring Legal Compliance in Private Money Brokering

Understanding Legal and Regulatory Frameworks

When it comes to private money brokering for residential real estate investments, it is crucial for beginning real estate investors to have a clear understanding of the legal and regulatory frameworks that govern this industry. Failure to comply with these laws and regulations can lead to severe consequences, including fines, legal disputes, and damage to your reputation. In this subchapter, we will delve into the essential aspects of the legal and regulatory frameworks you need to be aware of as a private money broker.

First and foremost, it is essential to understand that private money brokering involves raising funds from private individuals or entities to finance real estate investment projects. As a private money broker, you act as an intermediary between borrowers and lenders, facilitating the loan process. However, this activity is subject to various laws and regulations to protect both parties involved.

One of the primary legal considerations for private money brokering is licensing and registration. Depending on your jurisdiction, you may need to obtain specific licenses or registrations to operate as a private money broker legally. These requirements vary from state to state, so it is crucial to consult with a legal professional or regulatory body to ensure compliance.

Additionally, private money brokers must comply with anti-money laundering (AML) and know-your-customer (KYC) regulations. These regulations are designed to prevent money laundering, fraud, and terrorist financing. As a private money broker, you must implement robust AML and KYC procedures to verify the identities of both borrowers and lenders and ensure the legitimacy of the funds being exchanged.

Furthermore, private money brokers should familiarize themselves with the rules and regulations set forth by the Consumer Financial Protection Bureau (CFPB) and Securities and Exchange Commission (SEC). These agencies have specific guidelines pertaining to private lending and investment activities, and failure to comply with their regulations can result in severe penalties.

Lastly, it is vital to understand the legal aspects of loan documentation and contracts. As a private money broker, you will be responsible for drafting loan agreements, promissory notes, and other legal documents. It is crucial to ensure that these documents comply with all applicable laws and regulations to protect the interests of both parties involved.

In conclusion, understanding the legal and regulatory frameworks surrounding private money brokering for residential real estate investments is paramount for beginning real estate investors. By familiarizing yourself with licensing requirements, AML and KYC regulations, guidelines from regulatory bodies, and the legal aspects of loan documentation, you can operate within the bounds of the law and safeguard your investments and reputation. It is advisable to seek professional legal advice and stay updated on any changes in regulations to ensure ongoing compliance.

Navigating Licensing and Disclosure Requirements

When venturing into the world of private money brokering for residential real estate investments, it is crucial for beginning real estate investors to understand the licensing and disclosure requirements involved. This subchapter aims to demystify these aspects, providing a step-by-step guide to help you navigate through the process.

Licensing is an essential aspect of private money brokering. Depending on your location and the specific regulations governing real estate investments, you may be required to obtain a license to operate as a private money broker. It is vital to research and understand the licensing requirements in your area to ensure compliance with the law. Failing to do so can lead to legal repercussions and hinder your success in this field.

Disclosures are another critical aspect of private money brokering. As a beginning real estate investor, it is your responsibility to provide accurate and transparent information to potential investors. This includes disclosing any potential risks, conflicts of interest, fees, and commissions associated with the investment opportunity. Failure to disclose such information can lead to legal issues and damage your reputation in the industry.

To ensure compliance with licensing and disclosure requirements, it is advisable to consult with legal professionals who specialize in real estate investments. They can guide you through the process, ensuring that you meet all the necessary legal obligations. Additionally, attending seminars and workshops on private money brokering can provide valuable insights into the licensing and disclosure requirements specific to your niche.

When seeking licensing, it is crucial to gather all the necessary documentation, such as your educational qualifications, experience, and financial records. These documents will be evaluated to determine your eligibility for a license. Furthermore, understanding the fees associated with obtaining and maintaining a license is essential to plan your budget accordingly.

Regarding disclosures, it is essential to create a standardized disclosure document that encompasses all the necessary information. This document should be provided to potential investors before they commit to any investment opportunity. It is crucial to be transparent and disclose any potential risks involved, ensuring that investors are fully informed before making any financial commitments.

In conclusion, navigating licensing and disclosure requirements is an integral part of private money brokering for residential real estate investments. As a beginning real estate investor, it is crucial to understand and comply with the rules and regulations governing this field. By researching the licensing requirements, consulting legal professionals, and providing accurate disclosures, you can ensure a smooth and legally compliant journey into private money brokering.

Avoiding Common Legal Pitfalls

As a beginning real estate investor venturing into the world of private money brokering for residential real estate investments, it is crucial to be aware of and steer clear of common legal pitfalls. Understanding and adhering to the legal obligations and responsibilities associated with this niche is essential for your success and protection. In this subchapter, we will explore some of the most prevalent legal pitfalls and provide guidance on how to avoid them.

1. Licensing and Compliance: One of the primary legal pitfalls to avoid is operating without the necessary licenses and permits. Before engaging in private money brokering, it is vital to research and comply with the licensing requirements in your jurisdiction. Failure to do so can result in fines, legal complications, and reputational damage.

2. Disclosure and Documentation: When brokering private money deals, transparency and proper documentation are paramount. Ensure you have a thorough understanding of the disclosure requirements specific to your jurisdiction and include them in all relevant agreements. Accurate and complete documentation will protect both you and your investors from potential legal disputes.

3. Usury Laws: Usury laws vary from state to state and regulate the maximum interest rates that can be charged on loans. Familiarize yourself with the usury laws in your jurisdiction to avoid unwittingly charging excessive interest rates, which can lead to legal consequences and potentially invalidate your loan agreements.

4. Securities Laws: In some cases, brokering private money deals can involve the offering of securities. It is crucial to understand and comply with securities laws to avoid running afoul of regulations. Consult with a qualified attorney or seek guidance from regulatory bodies to ensure compliance.

5. Predatory Lending Practices: To maintain your reputation and avoid legal troubles, it is essential to steer clear of predatory lending practices. Conduct business ethically, provide transparent terms and conditions, and ensure borrowers fully understand the implications of their loans. Predatory lending practices can lead to legal action and damage your standing in the industry.

6. Privacy and Data Protection: As a private money broker, you will handle sensitive personal and financial information. Safeguarding this data is not only good business practice but also a legal obligation. Familiarize yourself with data protection laws and implement robust security measures to protect the privacy of your clients.

By being aware of these common legal pitfalls and taking proactive measures to avoid them, you can safeguard your investments, protect your reputation, and ensure a successful career in private money brokering for residential real estate investments. Remember, consulting with legal professionals experienced in real estate and financial regulations is always a wise decision to navigate the complex legal landscape.

Chapter 8: Maximizing Success in Private Money Brokering

Scaling Your Private Money Brokering Business

As a beginning real estate investor venturing into the niche of private money brokering for residential real estate investments, it is essential to understand how to scale your business for long-term success. Scaling your private money brokering business involves expanding your reach, increasing your deal flow, and building a solid reputation within the industry. In this subchapter, we will explore the key strategies and steps you need to take to scale your private money brokering business effectively.

1. Build a Strong Network: Scaling your business requires a robust network of potential investors, lenders, and real estate professionals. Attend networking events, join real estate investment clubs, and leverage social media platforms to connect with potential clients and partners. Building relationships and establishing trust will increase your chances of attracting more deals and referrals.

2. Develop a Marketing Plan: To scale your business, you need a solid marketing plan. Utilize digital marketing techniques such as creating a professional website, optimizing your online presence through search engine optimization (SEO), and leveraging social media advertising to attract potential investors and borrowers. Develop a consistent brand image and message to differentiate yourself from competitors.

3. Streamline Your Processes: Scaling your business involves optimizing your processes to handle increased deal flow efficiently. Implement technology solutions such as customer relationship management (CRM) software to manage your contacts and automate repetitive tasks. Develop standardized procedures for evaluating deals, conducting due diligence, and facilitating transactions to ensure consistency and efficiency.

4. Expand Your Offerings: Consider expanding your services beyond private money brokering. Explore opportunities to provide additional value to your clients, such as offering consulting services, real estate education, or access to a network of reliable contractors and vendors. Diversifying your offerings can attract more clients and increase your revenue streams.

5. Seek Partnerships and Collaborations: Scaling your private money brokering business can be accelerated by forming strategic partnerships and collaborations. Team up with experienced real estate investors, mortgage brokers, or real estate agents who can refer potential clients. Collaborate with professionals in related industries, such as property management or construction, to offer comprehensive solutions to your clients.

Remember, scaling your private money brokering business requires dedication, consistency, and a commitment to providing exceptional service. Continuously educate yourself on industry trends, stay updated on market conditions, and adapt your strategies accordingly. By implementing these strategies and taking calculated risks, you can position yourself for significant growth and success in the private money brokering industry.

Creating Win-Win Situations for Borrowers and Lenders

As a beginning real estate investor venturing into private money brokering for residential real estate investments, it is essential to understand the importance of creating win-win situations for both borrowers and lenders. In this subchapter, we will delve into the strategies and practices that can help you achieve this balance and foster successful partnerships in your real estate ventures.

First and foremost, it is crucial to recognize that both borrowers and lenders have unique goals and expectations. Borrowers seek financial assistance to fund their real estate projects, while lenders are looking for profitable investment opportunities. By understanding the motivations and desires of both parties, you can tailor your approach to ensure mutual satisfaction.

One key aspect to consider is the financial viability of the project. As a private money broker, you must thoroughly analyze the borrower's investment proposal to assess its potential for success. This involves evaluating the property's market value, potential returns, and the borrower's ability to repay the loan. By conducting due diligence and providing lenders with comprehensive information, you can instill confidence and increase the likelihood of securing financing.

Transparency and open communication are fundamental to building trust between borrowers and lenders. As a broker, it is your responsibility to act as a mediator and facilitate a clear understanding of the terms and conditions of the loan. This includes outlining the interest rates, repayment schedules, and any potential risks involved. By ensuring that both parties are fully aware of the agreement, you can mitigate misunderstandings and avoid future conflicts.

Flexibility is another crucial aspect of creating win-win situations. Real estate investments can be complex, and unexpected challenges may arise during the project's lifecycle. As a broker, you should be prepared to adapt and find solutions that benefit both borrowers and lenders. This may involve renegotiating terms or finding alternative sources of funding. By demonstrating your willingness to work through obstacles, you can strengthen relationships and foster long-term partnerships.

Lastly, it is important to emphasize the value of maintaining a strong reputation in the industry. Word-of-mouth recommendations and positive testimonials from satisfied borrowers and lenders can significantly enhance your credibility as a broker. By consistently delivering on your promises and prioritizing the interests of all parties involved, you can establish yourself as a trusted professional in the field of private money brokering.

In conclusion, creating win-win situations for borrowers and lenders is essential for success in private money brokering for residential real estate investments. By understanding their unique goals, fostering transparency, and demonstrating flexibility, you can forge strong partnerships and achieve mutually beneficial outcomes. Remember, building a positive reputation is paramount to your long-term success as a broker.

Learning from Experienced Private Money Brokers

As a beginning real estate investor venturing into the world of private money brokering for residential real estate investments, it is essential to seek guidance from experienced professionals who have already mastered this field. Learning from their expertise and experiences can provide valuable insights and help you navigate the intricacies of private money brokering.

Experienced private money brokers possess a wealth of knowledge about the industry, having successfully closed numerous deals and built strong relationships with lenders and investors. Their expertise can help you understand the nuances of private money brokering, enabling you to make informed decisions and maximize your chances of success.

One of the crucial aspects of learning from experienced private money brokers is understanding the strategies they employ to identify potential lenders and investors. These brokers have honed their skills in networking and building relationships within the real estate investment community. They can teach you how to identify the right lenders and investors for your specific needs, and how to approach them effectively.

Moreover, experienced brokers can guide you through the intricacies of structuring deals and negotiating terms. They can teach you how to analyze a potential investment opportunity, assess the risk factors, and present it in a compelling manner to lenders and investors. This knowledge is invaluable when it comes to securing the funding you need for your real estate projects.

Learning from experienced private money brokers also provides an opportunity to understand the legal and regulatory aspects of private money brokering. These brokers can guide you through the legal requirements, paperwork, and compliance issues involved in brokering private money deals. This knowledge is essential to ensure that your transactions are conducted in a lawful and ethical manner.

Additionally, experienced brokers can share their insights into the current market trends and industry practices. They can educate you about the various financing options available in the market, such as hard money loans, private loans, and crowdfunding. By staying updated on the latest trends and strategies, you can stay ahead of the competition and make informed investment decisions.

In conclusion, learning from experienced private money brokers is a crucial step for beginning real estate investors looking to venture into private money brokering for residential real estate investments. Their expertise, strategies, and knowledge can provide you with a solid foundation to succeed in this field. So, seek out these professionals, absorb their wisdom, and apply it to your own real estate investment journey.

Chapter 9: Common Challenges and How to Overcome Them

Dealing with Rejection and Overcoming Obstacles

As a beginning real estate investor venturing into the niche of private money brokering for residential real estate investments, it is crucial to understand that rejection and obstacles are inevitable parts of this journey. In this subchapter, we will delve into the strategies and mindset needed to overcome these challenges and achieve success in private money brokering.

Rejection is a common occurrence in any business, but it can be particularly disheartening when you are starting out in real estate investments. It is essential to remember that rejection is not personal, but rather a part of the learning process. Each rejection brings you closer to a potential yes. Maintain a positive mindset and view rejection as an opportunity for growth and improvement.

To deal with rejection effectively, it is important to analyze what went wrong and learn from it. Was it a lack of preparation or a misalignment of goals? Evaluate your approach and make necessary adjustments. Seek feedback from experienced investors or mentors to gain insights into how you can better present your investment opportunities.

Overcoming obstacles is another vital aspect of private money brokering. Challenges may arise in multiple forms, such as financial constraints, regulatory hurdles, or even personal doubts. To tackle these obstacles, it is crucial to have a well-defined plan and a strong support system.

Develop a clear strategy for addressing each obstacle you encounter. Break down the problem into manageable steps and create a timeline for accomplishing them. Seek advice from seasoned investors who have faced similar obstacles and successfully overcome them. Remember, obstacles are not roadblocks but rather opportunities to learn and grow.

Maintaining a positive mindset and perseverance are key to overcoming obstacles. Surround yourself with like-minded individuals who can provide support and encouragement. Join real estate investment clubs or online communities where you can connect with others facing similar challenges. Sharing experiences and learning from others can provide valuable insights and help you stay motivated during tough times.

In conclusion, rejection and obstacles are an inherent part of the private money brokering journey for beginning real estate investors. By viewing rejection as an opportunity for growth and learning, and by developing a clear strategy and a supportive network to tackle obstacles, you can overcome these challenges and achieve success in this niche. Stay focused, stay determined, and remember that each rejection brings you one step closer to achieving your real estate investment goals.

Managing Cash Flow and Financial Risks

One of the most critical aspects of becoming a successful real estate investor is understanding how to effectively manage cash flow and mitigate financial risks. In this subchapter, we will delve into the essential strategies and techniques that beginning real estate investors need to know when it comes to private money brokering for residential real estate investments.

Cash flow management is the lifeblood of any real estate venture. Without a solid understanding of how to effectively manage your cash flow, your investments can quickly turn into a financial nightmare. To begin with, it is crucial to create a comprehensive budget that outlines all your income and expenses related to your investment properties. This will help you track and monitor your cash flow, enabling you to make informed decisions about your investments.

Furthermore, it is essential to develop a contingency plan to address potential financial risks. Real estate investments are subject to various risks, including market fluctuations, unexpected repairs, and vacancies. By having a contingency plan in place, you can mitigate these risks and ensure that your cash flow remains steady.

Another crucial aspect of managing cash flow and financial risks is understanding the importance of maintaining adequate reserves. Building up a reserve fund is essential to cover unexpected expenses or periods of low cash flow. It is recommended to set aside a portion of your rental income each month to build up this reserve fund. By doing so, you will be prepared for any unforeseen circumstances and avoid financial strain.

Additionally, it is vital to continuously educate yourself on financial management strategies and stay informed about the real estate market. The more knowledge you have, the better equipped you will be to make sound financial decisions and minimize risks.

In conclusion, managing cash flow and financial risks is a crucial aspect of private money brokering for residential real estate investments. By creating a comprehensive budget, developing a contingency plan, maintaining adequate reserves, and continuously educating yourself, you will be well on your way to becoming a successful real estate investor. Remember, effective cash flow management and risk mitigation are essential for long-term financial stability and success in the real estate market.

Adapting to Market Changes and Trends

In the ever-changing world of real estate investing, it is crucial for beginning investors to understand the importance of adapting to market changes and trends. The ability to stay ahead of the curve and adjust your strategies accordingly can make all the difference in achieving success in private money brokering for residential real estate investments. In this subchapter, we will delve into the key principles and strategies to help you navigate market shifts and capitalize on emerging trends.

The real estate market is dynamic and influenced by a wide range of factors, such as economic conditions, interest rates, demographic changes, and government policies. As a beginning investor, it is essential to stay informed and regularly analyze market data to identify patterns and anticipate future trends. This involves monitoring local and national real estate reports, attending industry conferences and networking events, and engaging with experienced professionals in the field.

One important trend to consider is the growing demand for sustainable and eco-friendly properties. With increasing awareness about climate change and environmental conservation, many investors are seeking to align their investments with these values. As a private money broker, you can tap into this trend by connecting investors with developers who specialize in constructing energy-efficient and environmentally conscious homes.

Another trend to keep in mind is the rise of technology in the real estate industry. The advent of online platforms and mobile apps has revolutionized the way properties are marketed, purchased, and managed. As a beginning investor, it is crucial to embrace these technological advancements and leverage them to your advantage. This may involve using virtual reality tours to showcase properties to potential investors or utilizing data analytics to identify lucrative investment opportunities.

Furthermore, the current market conditions and economic climate may require you to adapt your financing strategies. As interest rates fluctuate, it is important to stay updated on the best financing options available. This could involve exploring alternative financing methods, such as crowdfunding or peer-to-peer lending, to secure the necessary funds for your real estate investments.

In conclusion, adapting to market changes and trends is a fundamental aspect of private money brokering for residential real estate investments. By staying informed, embracing emerging trends, and adjusting your strategies accordingly, you can position yourself as a successful beginning investor in this dynamic industry. Remember to continuously educate yourself, network with industry professionals, and be open to innovative approaches to financing and property management.

Chapter 10: The Future of Private Money Brokering

Emerging Opportunities and Trends in Private Money Brokering

In recent years, private money brokering has gained significant traction as an alternative financing option for residential real estate investments. As a beginning real estate investor, it is crucial to stay abreast of the emerging opportunities and trends in this field to maximize your chances of success. This subchapter aims to demystify the latest developments in private money brokering, equipping you with the knowledge needed to navigate this ever-evolving landscape.

One of the emerging opportunities in private money brokering is the increasing popularity of online platforms and crowdfunding. These platforms provide a convenient and efficient way for real estate investors to connect with potential private lenders. With just a few clicks, investors can present their projects and secure funding from a network of investors. This trend has opened up new avenues for those seeking private money to finance their residential real estate investments.

Furthermore, as traditional lending institutions continue to tighten their lending criteria, private money brokering has become an even more attractive option for real estate investors. Private lenders are often more flexible in their lending requirements, allowing investors with less-than-perfect credit or limited financial history to secure loans. This presents a unique opportunity for beginning investors who may not yet have established a strong financial track record.

Another trend worth noting is the increasing use of technology in private money brokering. Real estate investors can now leverage various software and tools to streamline the loan application and approval process, making it faster and more efficient. These technologies also enable investors to conduct thorough due diligence on potential private lenders, ensuring they are working with reputable and trustworthy individuals or organizations.

In addition to these emerging opportunities, it is vital to stay informed about the latest trends in private money brokering. This includes understanding the current market rates, terms, and conditions for private loans. By keeping an eye on these trends, you can negotiate more favorable terms with private lenders and secure the best financing options for your residential real estate investments.

As a beginning real estate investor, embracing these emerging opportunities and staying informed about the latest trends in private money brokering can give you a competitive edge. By leveraging online platforms, utilizing technology, and understanding market trends, you can unlock new financing options and increase your chances of success in the world of real estate investing.

Leveraging Technology for Increased Efficiency

In today's fast-paced world, technology has become an integral part of our lives, transforming the way we work and conduct business. For beginning real estate investors looking to venture into private money brokering for residential real estate investments, leveraging technology can significantly increase efficiency and help streamline processes. In this subchapter, we will explore the various ways technology can be harnessed to optimize your private money brokering efforts.

One of the key benefits of incorporating technology into your real estate investment strategy is the ability to streamline and automate time-consuming tasks. Traditional methods of securing private money for real estate deals often involved lengthy paperwork, manual calculations, and countless hours spent on phone calls and meetings. However, with the advent of digital tools and platforms, you can now automate these processes, saving both time and effort.

One such technology that can revolutionize your private money brokering journey is online crowdfunding platforms. These platforms allow you to connect with potential investors, showcase your real estate investment opportunities, and streamline the funding process. By utilizing these platforms, you can reach a larger audience and attract more investors, ultimately increasing your chances of securing private money for your residential real estate investments.

Additionally, technology can also help you manage and organize your real estate deals more efficiently. Real estate investment management software provides you with a centralized platform to track and monitor your investments, analyze data, and generate reports. This not only simplifies the management process but also allows you to make informed decisions based on accurate and up-to-date information.

Furthermore, technology can empower you to conduct due diligence more effectively. With online databases and tools, you can access property records, conduct background checks on potential borrowers or investors, and verify property values. This digital approach not only saves time but also minimizes the risk of errors and oversights.

Lastly, leveraging technology can also enhance your communication and networking capabilities. Social media platforms, real estate forums, and online communities provide you with opportunities to connect with other real estate investors, private lenders, and industry professionals. By actively engaging in these digital spaces, you can expand your network, gain valuable insights, and potentially form strategic partnerships.

In conclusion, technology is a powerful tool that can revolutionize the private money brokering process for beginning real estate investors. By incorporating online platforms, investment management software, and digital networking, you can increase efficiency, streamline operations, and ultimately achieve success in your residential real estate investments. Embrace technology and leverage its immense potential to take your private money brokering efforts to new heights.

Continuous Learning and Professional Growth in the Industry

As a beginning real estate investor venturing into the world of private money brokering for residential real estate investments, one of the key factors that will determine your success is your commitment to continuous learning and professional growth. In this subchapter, we will delve into the importance of staying updated with industry trends and the various strategies you can adopt to enhance your knowledge and skills.

The real estate industry is ever-evolving, and being aware of the latest market trends and investment strategies is essential for making informed decisions. Continuous learning allows you to stay ahead of the curve, identify lucrative investment opportunities, and mitigate potential risks. By constantly expanding your knowledge base, you will be better equipped to analyze market conditions, evaluate potential investments, and negotiate favorable deals.

There are numerous resources available to help you in your journey of continuous learning. Start by immersing yourself in real estate literature, both classic and contemporary, to gain a solid understanding of the industry's foundations. In addition to books, there are countless online courses, webinars, podcasts, and videos that offer valuable insights from experienced professionals. Consider joining real estate investment clubs or networking groups to connect with like-minded individuals who can share their experiences and knowledge.

Attending industry conferences and seminars is another great way to stay updated on the latest trends and build your network. These events provide opportunities to learn from experts in the field, participate in workshops, and engage in meaningful discussions with fellow investors. Surrounding yourself with successful and knowledgeable individuals will not only inspire you but also open doors to potential partnerships and mentorship opportunities.

Investing in your professional growth also involves acquiring specific skills related to private money brokering. This may include learning how to effectively communicate and build relationships with potential investors, understanding the legal and regulatory aspects of the industry, or developing negotiation and financial analysis skills.

Lastly, never underestimate the power of hands-on experience. Actively seek out opportunities to apply what you have learned, whether it's through shadowing experienced brokers, working as an intern, or even starting with small-scale investments. Practical experience will deepen your understanding of the industry and help you refine your strategies.

In conclusion, continuous learning and professional growth are crucial for beginning real estate investors in the niche of private money brokering for residential real estate investments. By staying updated with industry trends, expanding your knowledge, and honing your skills, you can position yourself for success in this dynamic and competitive industry. Embrace the mindset of a lifelong learner, and your journey towards becoming a successful private money broker will be paved with opportunities and achievements.

Conclusion: Your Journey as a Private Money Broker

Congratulations! You have reached the end of this comprehensive guide on private money brokering for residential real estate investments. By now, you should have a deep understanding of what it takes to become a successful private money broker and how to navigate the world of real estate investing.

Throughout this book, we have covered various aspects of private money brokering, from understanding the basics of real estate investing to building relationships with lenders and investors. We have provided you with step-by-step instructions, practical tips, and valuable insights to help you kickstart your career as a private money broker.

As a beginning real estate investor, you have now unlocked a powerful tool that will propel you towards financial success. Private money brokering allows you to access the necessary funds to invest in profitable real estate deals, even if you don't have a substantial amount of capital yourself. By connecting borrowers with private lenders, you can earn lucrative commissions and build a strong network in the real estate industry.

In conclusion, this book has equipped you with the knowledge, tools, and strategies needed to excel as a private money broker in the residential real estate investment market. Remember to continuously educate yourself, adapt to changes, and build strong relationships. With dedication and hard work, you can turn your passion for real estate into a thriving career as a private money broker. Good luck on your journey!

However, it is important to remember that success as a private money broker is not guaranteed overnight. It requires patience, persistence, and continuous learning. Real estate markets can be unpredictable, and the lending landscape is constantly evolving. To stay ahead in this industry, you must stay updated with the latest market trends, regulations, and investment strategies.

In addition to that, building and nurturing relationships will be crucial to your success. Cultivate trust with lenders, investors, and borrowers, and always deliver on your promises. Reputation is everything in the real estate world, and a good word from a satisfied client can open doors to countless opportunities.

Lastly, don't be afraid to seek guidance and mentorship from experienced private money brokers or real estate investors. Networking with industry professionals can provide you with invaluable advice and insights that can fast-track your journey towards becoming a successful private money broker.

MR. REAL ESTATE.DON
"I MAKE THEM AN OFFER, THEY CAN'T REFUSE!"

Private Money Brokering Demystified: A Step-by-Step Guide for Novice Real Estate Investors